# About the Music © 2010

We all love the melodies of Christmas. With each passing year, however, the heartwarming sounds of our childhood carols are increasingly drowned out by the noise of cash registers and commercials. Each autumn the neon signs on every corner blinking "XMAS SALE!" seem switched on earlier than the year before—the meaning of Christmas relegated (again) to an even smaller space in society.

Jeff Bjorck's fifth Pure Piano CD, *The Wondrous Gift,* is his somewhat about-face response to these forward-marching materialistic trends. He takes you back to a simpler time, when the term "Merry Christmas" was still considered a warm greeting.

The classic carols featured on this CD will bring listeners floods of memories. As he did on his last CD, *This I Know: Ageless Hymns of Faith*, Jeff brings unique interpretative arrangements to each of the dozen selections while making sure to pay tribute to the original melodies. Although recorded in 2010, many of the selections he's been playing for years. Jeff loves them all, and each has a story to tell. The sonic results provide listeners with music suitable for many occasions, from intimate holiday gatherings to Sunday morning preludes to personal times of nostalgic reflection.

Jeff's Pure Piano Music has been drawing avid listeners from around the world for the last 13 years, thanks to an Internet that makes music globally accessible. The Internet has also given Jeff ready access to his listeners, and before choosing the pieces for this CD, he polled them regarding their favorite carols. This collaborative effort resulted in a cross-section of carols for *The Wondrous Gift* truly loved by all who love Christmas as well as Jeff's music. "I'm very grateful for my listeners," Jeff says. "It's my heartfelt wish that this new music brings each one of them joy, nostalgia, and a reminder of Christmas' true meaning, both this year and for many years to come."

One particularly happy outcome was that Jeff's favorite carol, "O Holy Night," was the overwhelming favorite among those polled. Whereas many arrangements of this piece tend to transform it into a rousing anthem, Jeff's arrangement preserves the quiet peace and awe doubtless felt by Mary, Joseph, and the shepherds on that first Christmas Eve. Other selections, such as "Coventry Carol" create a space for sadness when loved ones are no longer present to celebrate Christmas with us. Still others, such as "O Come All Ye Faithful" and "Come, Thou Long-Expected Jesus," reflect the exuberant anticipation experienced by so many at this time of year.

*The Wondrous Gift* is sure to create a sense of wonder that echoes the angels' joyous proclamation that first Christmas: "Glory to God in the highest, and on earth peace, good will toward all."

*Turn to the back of this book for the stories behind the music!*

# THE WONDROUS GIFT
## *A Pure Piano Christmas by*
# JEFF BJORCK: Solo Piano Songbook

## TABLE OF CONTENTS

# O Little Town of Bethlehem

From the solo piano CD *The Wondrous Gift: A Pure Piano Christmas*
Available from *Purepiano.com*

Lewis H. Redner, 1868
Arranged for piano by Jeffrey Bjorck

# O Holy Night

From the solo piano CD *The Wondrous Gift: A Pure Piano Christmas*
Available from *Purepiano.com*

Adolphe Adam
Arranged for piano by Jeffrey Bjorck

# What Child Is This?

From the solo piano CD *The Wondrous Gift: A Pure Piano Christmas*
Available from *Purepiano.com*

16th c. English melody
Arranged for piano by Jeffrey Bjorck

# O Come All Ye Faithful

From the solo piano CD *The Wondrous Gift: A Pure Piano Christmas*
Available from *Purepiano.com*

John Francis Wade, 1751
Arranged for piano by Jeffrey Bjorck

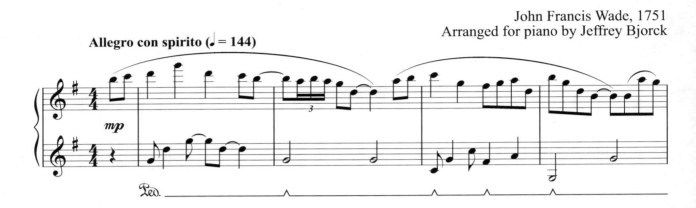

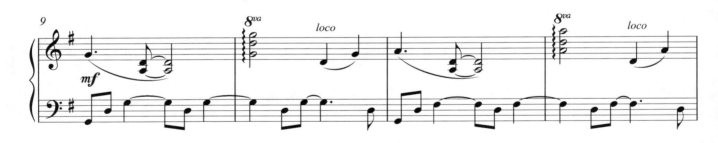

# Hark, the Herald Angels Sing

From the solo piano CD *The Wondrous Gift: A Pure Piano Christmas*
Available from *Purepiano.com*

Felix Mendelssohn, 1840
Arranged for piano by Jeffrey Bjorck

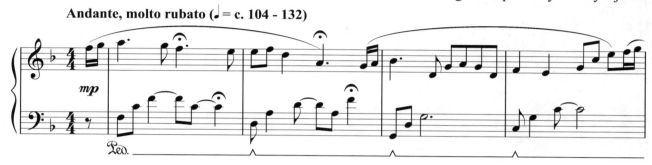

# Silent Night

From the solo piano CD *The Wondrous Gift: A Pure Piano Christmas*
Available from *Purepiano.com*

Music by Franz Xaver Gruber, c. 1820
Arranged for piano by Jeffrey Bjorck

# It Came Upon a Midnight Clear

From the solo piano CD *The Wondrous Gift: A Pure Piano Christmas*
Available from *Purepiano.com*

Richard S. Willis, 1850
Arranged for piano by Jeffrey Bjorck

# Away In A Manger

From the solo piano CD *The Wondrous Gift: A Pure Piano Christmas*
Available from *Purepiano.com*

Music by James R. Murray, c. 1887
Arranged for piano by Jeffrey Bjorck

Purepiano.com

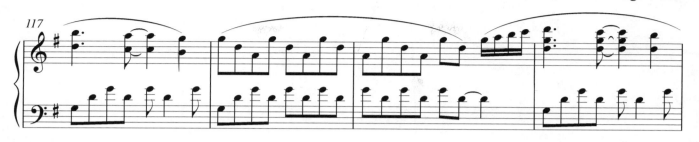

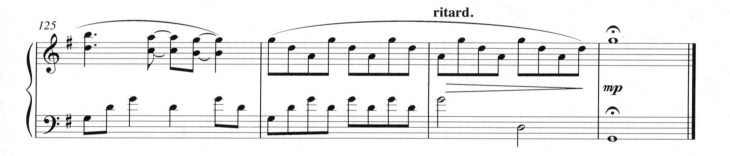

# Bring A Torch, Jeannette Isabella

From the solo piano CD *The Wondrous Gift: A Pure Piano Christmas*
Available from *Purepiano.com*

Traditional
Arranged for piano by Jeffrey Bjorck

# Coventry Carol

From the solo piano CD *The Wondrous Gift: A Pure Piano Christmas*
Available from *Purepiano.com*

Traditional
Arranged for piano by Jeffrey Bjorck

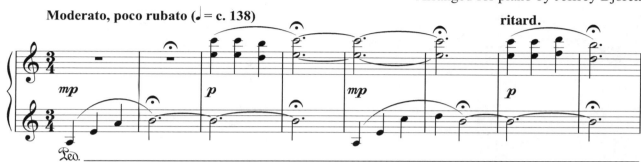

# O Come, O Come Emmanuel

From the solo piano CD *The Wondrous Gift: A Pure Piano Christmas*
Available from *Purepiano.com*

15th c. French melody
Arranged for piano by Jeffrey Bjorck

Purepiano.com

*O Come, O Come Emmanuel*, Jeffrey Bjorck

# Come, Thou Long Expected Jesus

From the solo piano CD *The Wondrous Gift: A Pure Piano Christmas*
Available from *Purepiano.com*

Rowland H. Prichard, 1830
Arranged for piano by Jeffrey Bjorck

***O Little Town of Bethlehem***: As with my previous CD of hymns, planning this project included a conversation with my friend, Dr. Richard J. Mouw, then president of Fuller Theological Seminary. Our love of the old songs also includes carols. When I asked for his favorite, he cited this piece, particularly because of the line: "The hopes and fears of all the years are met in thee tonight." I've always loved the beauty of stillness in this carol. And when reflecting on an appropriate title for this CD, my wife Sharon suggested I return to this song and another line: "How silently, how silently, the wondrous Gift is giv'n." Indeed, God not only sent us his greatest gift without a sound, but also wrapped this gift in the poverty and humility of a stable.

***O Holy Night***: Growing up, I believed that no one could sing this song better than Bing Crosby, most likely because Crosby was one of my father's heroes. As a result, Christmas is never complete without at least some time spent listening to Bing, which escorts me back to my earliest childhood memories. I also resonate with many of the lyrics. I can readily imagine "falling on my knees" if I had been one of the shepherds hearing the "angel voices." I have also experienced that "in all our trials, [Jesus] was born to be our friend." And I hope for the day when "in His name, all oppression shall cease."

***What Child Is This?***: I have often marveled at how perfectly the lyrics for this carol match the 16th century melody ("Greensleeves"), even though they were penned by William Dix hundreds of years later. The minor tones do evoke sadness, yet when paired with the lyrics, the combination inspires hope—strengthened by lyrics that also speak of Jesus' destiny on earth, where "nails, spear shall pierce him through, the cross be born for me, for you." I've long been struck by Christmas TV specials that omit all but the mildest lyrics from carols such as this one. Yet I agree with William Dix and many other carol writers that without Easter, Christmas would lose its meaning.

***O Come All Ye Faithful***: Christmas is also a time for exuberance, and for me, this carol epitomizes the joy of the season. As a child, singing this song in church prompted me to imagine what it might have been like if the baby Jesus had received a truly royal birthday celebration! With this in mind, I have intentionally arranged this piece to reflect the excitement and anticipation of Christmas. Indeed my favorite line is, "Yea, Lord, we greet thee, born this happy morning!"

***Hark! The Herald Angels Sing***: This carol is typically sung as a rousing anthem—fitting given Mendelssohn's triumphant lyrics and melodic march. I have found, however, that many Christmas carols emphasize either the triumphant joy of God incarnate or the gentle humility of the helpless infant, but not both. It occurred to me that deliberately softening the melody of this exultant carol might simultaneously produce these feelings in the listener. So I hope my arrangement beckons you to retain the majestic awe the shepherds felt when the angels appeared, while also remembering the baby, "Jesus, our Emmanuel," God with us.

***Silent Night***: Because I grew up in northern NJ, the concept of a white Christmas has been part of my cultural heritage, and I've always thought of snow as a perfect part of Christmas. Perhaps because there seems nothing more silent than new falling nighttime snow, I've always associated images of a fresh white blanket below twinkling stars whenever I heard this song. My intent with this arrangement was to emphasize that deep silence, doubtless broken by the baby's cries that first Christmas Eve. Because of Jesus, we can "sleep in heavenly peace," even in a noisy world.

***It Came Upon a Midnight Clear***: For me, this song is a close relative of "Silent Night," and for that reason I intentionally juxtaposed them. The lyrics also remind me of Charles M. Schultz's

1965 *A Charlie Brown Christmas*, in which Linus tells Charlie what "Christmas is all about." Linus echoes this song's lyrics, quoting the angels' proclamation, "Peace on the earth, good will to men, from Heaven's all-gracious King." Linus' recitation signifies for me the turning point for Charlie Brown in that TV special, just as these words signify the turning point in human history.

*Away in a Manger*: This carol has multiple melodies, and I've always loved them all. Since I couldn't choose one, I used two full melodies and portions of two others. This song has always struck me as a children's song, and it was apparently first published as such. Thus I attempted to create a childlike happiness and delicacy in this arrangement. Having said this, as a youth I was disturbed by the line, "But little Lord Jesus, no crying He makes," which made no sense to me. After all, this child grew up to be "a man of sorrows, acquainted with grief" (Isaiah 53: 3), and he certainly wept as an adult (John 11: 35). Why should he start life without healthy tears? Yes, Jesus is God, but he was also completely human and knows how we feel.

*Bring a Torch, Jeannette Isabella*: I first encountered this song in third or fourth grade when a classmate sang a Christmas concert solo. I was immediately captivated by the tune and lovely lyrics, which exhort all the stable inhabitants, "Hush! Hush!" so that baby Jesus can enjoy his first dreams. Thereafter, I rarely heard it because it was not part of the Protestant traditions of my childhood. Still, this age-old Catholic carol has remained with me, and its refrain always transports me to those early years.

*Coventry Carol*: At Christmas, we enjoy happy reunions with friends and family, but it is also a time when we often miss those no longer here. Indeed, from its beginning, Christmas has included sadness amidst joy. I have always been reminded of this truth by this somber carol, even though I did not know its lyrics. Indeed, over the years my awareness of sadness at Christmas has prompted me to reflect on what it must have been like for the parents who lost their infants in King Herod's massacre. (Shortly after Jesus birth, this tyrant had attempted to kill Jesus by destroying all the male children in Bethlehem under the age of two.) Then, while doing research for this CD, I was fascinated to learn that this carol is actually a lamenting lullaby for those babies. It's easy to quickly skim past this event to focus on Jesus and his parents' happy escape from Herod into Egypt, but the Bible does not skim. It speaks of "Rachel weeping for her children, refusing to be comforted" (Matthew 2: 18). So I've changed the major chord traditionally closing each verse to minor in tribute to "Rachel's children"—and to everyone who remembers departed loved ones at Christmas.

*O Come, O Come Emmanuel*: As just explained, "Coventry Carol" typically ends on a major note, but the reverse is true for this carol. Yet, for me, this carol speaks of a joyous hope because Jesus' birth enabled his death at Calvary, where he conquered sin and death. Among my favorite lyrics from this song are the lines, "Disperse the gloomy clouds of night, and death's dark shadows put to flight!" I'll say it again: Christmas is truly joyous because of Easter, when—in the ultimate sense—Christ removed the sting of death forever. Therefore I have chosen to close my arrangement on a major chord.

*Come, Thou Long-Expected Jesus*: I arranged the opening and closing chords of this piece to suggest Christmas bells ringing out with expectancy. The tune for these bells is intended to reflect traditional clock chimes. I wished to create the excited sense of anticipation, so often seen in children—and many adults—as they wait for Christmas to come each year. Yet, this song does not refer to waiting for Christmas; rather, it is a request for Jesus to come again and "raise us to Thy glorious throne." I am grateful for the gift of life here on earth, but my ultimate hope and yearning is for the day when all is made right—when Christ comes to bring his children home once for all, and Christmas joy begins for eternity.

15291174R00042